Crocodiles

By Alison Tibbitts and
Alan Roocroft

PUBLISHED BY
Capstone Press
Mankato, Minnesota USA

CIP
LIBRARY OF CONGRESS CATALOGING IN PUBLICATION DATA

Tibbitts, Alison.
    Crocodiles / by Alison Tibbitts and Alan Roocroft.
        p. cm. -- (Animals, animals, animals)
    Summary: Discusses the physical characteristics, behavior, and life cycle of crocodiles.

    ISBN 1-56065-102-4
    1. Crocodiles -- Juvenile literature. [1. Crocodiles.]
    I. Roocroft, Alan. II. Title. III. Series: Tibbitts, Alison.
    Animals, animals, animals.
    QL666.C925T53   1992
    597.98 -- dc20   92-11439
                                                               CIP
                                                               AC

Consultant:
Tom Schultz, Curator of Reptiles
Zoological Society of San Diego

Photo Credits:
Alison Tibbitts and Alan Roocroft: 3, 13, 17

Gregory C. Lepera: Cover photo, title page, 4, 7, 9, 14, 18, 21, 22, 25, 26, 29, 32, back cover

Casey Tibbitts: 10

Capstone Press
P.O. Box 669, Mankato, MN, U.S.A. 56002-0669

"There be dragons." These words were written across unexplored places on old maps. They spin images of sea monsters, dinosaurs, and giant reptiles. Such creatures are gone now.

Crocodiles still live. They have been on earth for two hundred million years. Dinosaurs were their cousins. Only crocodiles and their relatives, the alligators, survived the climate changes that killed other large reptiles. Birds are their closest living relatives today.

Crocodiles are lumpy, bumpy, and grumpy. Africans called them "the animal that kills while it is smiling." The ancient Greek city of Crocodilopolis honored them. A most famous "croc" ate Captain Hook's hand in the story of Peter Pan.

Crocodiles are **complex** when compared to other reptiles. Their brains and hearts are more developed. They have a **higher social order**. Many may live together and get along well. Two sometimes team up to hold and tear **prey** before sharing it.

Crocodiles are at home in warm, humid climates around the globe. This wide range of habitats has insured their survival. They like calm backwaters and avoid open seas.

Reptiles are **cold-blooded**. Their body temperature is controlled by heat from outside sources. If a crocodile is cold, he basks in the sun. If he is too warm, he finds shade. He rests with his mouth open to release excess body heat. He heads for the water when he is really hot or disturbed.

Many crocodiles are shy and avoid human contact. Australia's freshwater crocodiles are timid and afraid of man. They hide among the reeds under water for up to two hours at a time.

A few crocodiles attack if angered, especially while nesting. The only known man-eaters are Africa's Nile crocodile and Australia's salt water crocodile. Salt water crocodiles are the biggest and most dangerous in the world. They grow to 25 feet. That is the length of two small cars parked bumper to bumper.

Crocodiles' lives are affected by animals around them. In Africa, over a million **wildebeests** move from place to place every year. Baboons living along the shore announce their approach to the river. The crocodiles sink low in the water. Their eyes, ears, and nostrils are barely visible. They wait to snatch unsuspecting wildebeests.

Female crocodiles protect their nests. This makes the area safe for other breeding animals. Birds build homes in the walls of abandoned crocodile nests. The **hatchlings**' eggshells provide calcium for birds and fish.

Crocodiles know the meaning of each other's grunts, hisses, growls, and chirps. At times, one will rise halfway out of the water and slap his head on the surface. This noisy action tells an intruder, "Get lost. This is my territory."

One male makes the rules for the crocodiles along the riverbank. He decides who enters the area. Passing males must submit to his control. They arch their backs and raise their heads to show their throats. If they do not, the ruler will attack them.

Many people think "typical" crocodiles are in Eastern and Central Africa. In fact, there are twenty-one **species** in the world. Skulls, scales, and teeth tell which crocodiles belong to what family. Their length ranges from three to twenty-five feet. They weigh from twenty pounds to over two tons. Some may live a hundred years. Females can breed for over fifty years.

Crocodiles' heads have bumps and knobs. Bodies carry a hard leather covering. Backs have ridges. Sharp teeth lie outside the upper jaw when the mouth is closed. Crocodiles swing from side to side when they walk. They do not move up and down.

These reptiles catch prey by sneaking up on it. They glide like a floating log toward a possible meal. They may not have any luck. If they do, the prey is torn, crunched and gulped. Crocodiles cannot chew. They swallow stones to help grind food in their stomachs.

Crocodiles may eat once a week-or once a year. It depends on the food supply where the crocodiles live. It also matters how fast their bodies use food. Many species eat small rodents, birds and fish. Large crocodiles grab whatever they can.

Believe it or not, crocodiles are good parents. They breed in shallow water after weeks of courtship. One month later, the female gathers plant materials and builds a nest, or she digs a deep hole in the sand. She lays up to eighty eggs the size of oval tennis balls. She fills up the hole. She lies down on top to protect the nest. Sun and **decaying** plants **incubate** the eggs. She rarely eats. She leaves briefly to cool off in the hottest part of the day. Predators think twice about coming near cranky nesting crocodiles.

Chirping "yelps" alert her to uncover the nest about three months later. This work is long and tiring. Her stubby legs are not shaped for digging. She keeps going. She knows her babies' chirps from others nearby.

The female rakes the babies gently into a special pouch in her mouth. She flips some to get them inside. **Sensors** below her teeth tell her if she needs to help any of the eggs to open.

She snorts as she carries her babies to their water nursery. She may make four or five trips. She hurries because her nest is unguarded while she is gone. The chirping can be heard by predators like monitor lizards, mongooses, and wading birds waiting nearby.

Water nurseries have clumpy weeds to hide the hatchlings. The babies feed off their **yolk sacs** at first. They soon learn to catch frogs, insects, and fish. The female "baby-sits" for several weeks. Hatchlings climb on her as she basks in the sun or lies in the water. She is patient and does not harm them. Male crocodiles can be gentle and protective with the babies too.

Crocodiles have been hunted for their hides for years. Now the reptiles are in danger of **extinction**. Some countries try to protect them. Illegal poaching happens anyway.

American alligators, who are closely related to crocodiles, almost became extinct years ago due to poachers who killed them for their skins.

Crocodile farming is a new idea to help solve the poaching problem. American alligators, who are closely related to crocodiles, have increased in number through farming. This success means they are no longer threatened with extinction. Hides from these farms are sold legally to people making leather goods. **Poachers** have fewer places to sell their stolen hides. This idea may save an ancient creature still walking the earth after two hundred million years.

GLOSSARY / INDEX

Cold-blooded: animal whose temperature is controlled by conditions outside his body (page 8)

Complex: many small details, related parts make up the whole (page 6)

Decaying: falling apart, breaking down (page 19)

Extinction: ceasing to exist, no longer living (page 27)

Hatchlings: babies who have come out of their shell recently (page 12)

Higher social order: definite organization where all members know their position and role in the group (page 6)

Incubate: to keep eggs warm until they hatch (page 19)

Poachers: people who break the law to kill animals and steal their body parts to sell (page 28)

Prey: animals hunted and killed by another animal for food (page 6)

Sensors: nerves that send messages to the brain (page 20)

Species: animals that are alike and can reproduce among themselves but not with other species (page 15)

Wildebeests: animals in the antelope family who live and graze on Africa's plains and open woodlands. A wildebeest is also called a gnu (page 11)

Yolk sac: the part of the egg that surrounds and holds the yolk while it develops into the animal (page 24)